The Inanity of Music & Wings

🌿 POEMS BY 🌿

ZACHARY MICHAEL JACK

NEW BUFFALO PRESS

1ST WORLD LIBRARY

1st WORLD LIBRARY
Literary Society

Austin • Fairfield • Delhi

Acknowledgements

Grateful acknowledgment is made to the editors of the following publications, in which some of these poems, some in different versions, appeared: *Borderlands Texas Poetry Review*: "Only the Lovers Warm the Face of Death"; *Cider Press Review*: "How Good It Was, Just Then, to Hear Elvis's High Wail," "Esperanza Arrives to Silence in the Sprawling Garden" (published as "Chapter II" and "Chapter III" respectively); *Exit 13*: "We Are Always More or Less in Love with the Musician" (published as "I Am Making Order with All the Indignation of a Snubbed God); *Northern Stars*: "The Retired General Still Wears His Fatigues," "I Return, a Falcon-headed God, a Blaze of Feathers," "The Fifth Grade, Mostly Anglo, Mostly Angelic, Leans in, Listens" (published collectively as "El Pajaro's Book of Desires"); *Poetry Motel*: "Bird Afterword" (published as "You Never Know"); *Sierra Nevada Review*: "Dramatis Personae," "The Mask of Juan Orta, Maestro, Bled from Its Eyes with Impunity," "Bird on What Must Be Broken," "Christ in the Square Touches Them Like a Flower," "I Read to Stave off Cravings. Bird Thins the Clouds" (published collectively as "The Book of Desires"); *Third Coast*: "Bird, on Lesser Gods," "Bird on Other Worlds" (published as "It Might Be Worth Your Knowing," and "Reader, I Don't Know Much About Tunisia" respectively); and the *Valparaiso Poetry Review*: "Postcard 1955: An Incendiary Year in the *Register*, Claiming," "Postcard 1959: There's Khrushchev and There's Grandfather" (published as "Postcard 1959: Coon Rapids, Iowa. Halcyon Days").

Thanks to New Buffalo Press and First World Library for making this book possible; to Niall Bracken and Bruce Smith for their abiding friendship and care; to Ben Gunsberg, Mark Ehling, and T.J. Beitelman for their good hearts and good words; and to my family, for their spirit.

for Edward Lee Jack and Julia Mae Jack
for that good world

Contents

III.

The Inanity of Music
& Wings

O lyric Love, half angel and half bird,
And all a wonder and a wild desire.

—Browning, *The Ring and the Book*

Dramatis Personae

Bird, who won't sit still, not for a minute, lights
in the mind. *Esperanza*, who does the gardening,
rights the upset, wilds the rest. *Diego* ministers
in the hotel, idles in the garden Bird claims
for his own. *Francisco*, revolutionary cheesemaker
and extra. *Spider*, who occasionally comes and goes.
Conquistador, the Bogeyman, god for an interlude.
Myself, aped ascetic and protagonist—page-turner
of The Book of Desires Bird proffers like gospel.
Grandfather, the one at home in the twilight.
Cat, who fancies herself a queen. *Khrushchev*,
the one with the plan for the virgin lands. *Elvis*,
the old ravenhair riding the shortwaves. *Tom Selleck*,
after all, the image of man. In the end, of course, desire
wears a mustache.

How Good It Was, Just Then, To Hear Elvis's High Wail

How good it was, just then, to hear Elvis's high wail
on the radio—Blue Moon's falsetto and spare guitar—
while the lost souls of Mexico, truer Graceland,
sidestep Trinitrons.

(The random American arrives—tennis shoes, ball cap,
legs—white clouds brightening against dark ones. It will mean
rain of course, and all of us would rather hide
under the elephantine arch than basket our heads and brave it).

The fogged-up windows keep everyone inside.
Cervasas atone for the garish red tables.
The night, thus unfolding, becomes a matter of probability.
It's hit and miss.

On *Calle Ibarra*, the street I've pronounced my own,
I'll know by the way the women eat their corn off its stick,
which way to go, where to look—
all subtleties of choice and taste, all subvocals of language.

I couldn't say one thing to the taxi driver, but when Heartbreak
Hotel came on, we looked at one another in ways that said
I'm calling Coke universal. I'm calling the auspicious clearing,
late in the afternoon, temporary relief.

So seldom do the birds stop chattering. So rarely
is the stomach perfectly finished off; it complains. Thus,
the square at night is a circus of appetites, and the bossa nova
just foreign enough to whet them.

Esperanza Arrives to Silence in the Sprawling

Esperanza arrives to silence in the sprawling
garden, weariness creeping, by afternoon,
across her sun-lined face. At night, her singing—
loud, clear, and perfectly unexpected—rings the fluted glass.
Father Diego, whistled in from down the street, strums
alongside, their sudden collision of selves making both divine.

Of course I love the gardener—Esperanza, Spanish *hope*.
While we wait, tell me again how, in the Azores,
men wear their hats in the hot, hot sun,
how, along the promenade, women don bright dresses
800 miles from anywhere. The snapdragons, when they wave,
look a deck of languid good-byes. Esperanza, I've romanced
the tabula rasa, made good the theory of the archipelago.

Santa Maria! The thrill of the body's mooring. The exclusive
eating of canned fish and pineapple, that futile,
month's long embroidery. Bird and I listen dumbly,
sobered by witness, then leave Diego and his angel
their wineglow and metaphysics. Bird knows
I am not fit. Of course you love the gardener,
he says. *Translator, ocean, bridge.*

Last Night, My First in the Mission

Last night, my first in the mission—
long night of pinion, fire I couldn't get close enough to.
Moth so loud at the ceiling I guessed it might be Bird.
The bridge between this world and the next, Bird says,
may not be Mexico; could be Woman.
The vase has hips you might hold, the lime
a perfect roundness you have already felt.

The tree in the courtyard bends with its passion.
The glass constantly rattles at the edge of its abyss.
Where the tree branches, close to the ground,
your future grows inexact. You try to cross
your right leg over your left, but feel all bundled up,
hiding something. You must have miscomprehended
your left-footed life to be still in bed, Bird says, teeth flashing.

Days When I Fight off Sleep Like Bear, I Promise Myself

Days when I fight off sleep like Bear, I promise myself:
No rest until the rain begins—such small, barometric
incentives for the grassy field, for the body's warm trunk.
A quick overarching sky at midnight traces the thigh
muscling upward, the lovely breast-fall. Bird is relentless.
Write it, he says, hovering, *desire's first page*—serpent slow
down the middle of the forehead, night sweat, edge of leaf.

Somehow I find my way inside and say, This house isn't mine.
This mission is someone else's—a pair of glassblowers high
on a moonlit lake, a company of monks at matins. In church
I could see where the glass had been reenvisioned, where,
in the tile, the heads of gods emerged blue and nebulous.
Never would I build so inspired, so light as this. Galleries
all over the world—New York, London—fill me with the same
spirit: green or blue, neither color my sea.

Because I Helped You down with It, Diego, Father

Because I helped you down with it, Diego, Father,
my hands smell of lime, the way they might
smell of woman warmly reached inside.
I carry the scent all day, lusting after the statuette's
public bosom. I would have helped the ferns unfurl, too,
but the *policia's* firm hand drew me away: the face
of authority so young these days, so unblinking. I feel naked
as before. I build a fire, go to the mirror, flames still
licking my fleece. I want to know again, like some
feverish child, fire's thoughts—the body's changing
shape, becoming elastic in the room. Fire in the hole!
Fire in the head! The way, in the hills, a woman's deep
wanting turns lava back at the chapel door. On her knees,
how she wills that god-island. The way, at 10, good farm
work burned whole afternoons, made us hot in our skins.
And evening kept coming—too soon—not at all
accidentally, and we pushed back, touched already
by its cooly intentional hands.

The Mask of Juan Orta, Maestro, Bleeds from Its Eyes

The mask of Juan Orta, maestro, bleeds from its eyes
with impunity. Oh, be indiscreet! I say,
and the clouds well up with moon behind.
The plasterers come out with trowel and lime, cement the haunt.

The night brings shorter skirts and teens by threes,
while the moon goes suddenly shy and won't come out.
People grow cold and hug whatever's weakest in themselves.
I alone escort a thousand illicit thoughts.

Yellow Woman emerges from Dr. Augosto's
House of Dental Fire, holding her jaw. It is a fine jaw.
The rain slips off the roof just as designed.
Jaguar Woman, for once, wills herself to be led.

Everyone else hurries home, wall-hugging.
There is one leaf, in particular, that can't
get enough, wagging its green tongue at me.
In back of the café, the child, the surfer's son,

stabs cork. His mother doesn't know
what to do with him, his butter knife raised,
his eyes wilding. His black hair escapes her
completely. On saxophone Jocko climbs the scales

and outside it continues rain. *Stormy Weather.*
Skylark, have you anything to say to me?
In the corner, a man expertly tongues his wife's
ring finger, slipping me a look that says, Please . . .

A moment's peace! Denied their proper due,
of course the fingers take exception. The married one
would know, would have studied every inch
with the confidence of a scholar.

I Read to Stave off Cravings. Bird Thins the Clouds

I read to stave off cravings. Bird thins the clouds
of a few hundred starlets. What should be fire
is only smoke. *Mi solo*, I keep saying in the market,
Mi solo en esta grande casa, waving my pointer finger,
ears bandshelled for a mate—hypotheses
for how I hate myself grown old, how others achieve
more spectacular results: Heron commits adultery.
Starfish loses an arm, makes another sweet, sticky gift.
So the curve on the road to city of Uropan slips me
back into the sleeping Esperanza, she wearing her
"I work best alone" face. Attraction: the way
the moon used to follow, mile after country mile.
Come on! She's old enough to be your mother . . .
Iris in the garden back home with her sloppy tongue.
At that, Lizard on the leaf ingratiates himself, gets obscure
as an academician. Therefore, the moon carries on, careful
along the hairpins.

The Big-haired Man at the Corner Table (Rumored)

The big-haired man at the corner table (rumored)
is a movie star, *estrella*. Two brothers race their toy cars
up and down the bench in the plaza where the trench-coated
American breaks down, drinks a cup of *atole*, pitches
herself an ecstatic fit.

The economics of coffee! *Estupendo*!
Were she long here, she'd discover Franscisco, the cheesemaker,
makes revolutionary gouda. She'd learn the German restaurateur
who stole Francisco's recipe betrayed her also, then closed
the factory down.

In spite of myself, I sneer at the tourists, knowing
the little things that offer themselves, otherwise, only
as surfaces. Yet I, too, am a cipher, the one who leaves
the mission house once, twice a day in my fleece, letting fall
heels of bread.

Sketching Don Vasco's statue, each day a new slant on the self,
same. I manage to animate the old priest—wheeling
on his stony feet to offer absolutions. Today, Don Vasco, I believe
I am burdenless. I blend well into the fountain around which,
it seems, we are all stars.

All along the Street—Cars Our Fathers Bought Us

All along the street—cars our fathers bought us:
Darts, Mavericks, Pintos—the just good enough.
Now, digging in our backpacks for a train schedule,

(*where is it, damn it!*) we would gladly take them
for a spin, give them a second
chance, zooming north, cacti recalling

those awkward, too-human
shadows: faceless but solid. Predictably there.
Part of the landscape meant to be a moving reel

for us, a background against which
we judged progress.
Elvis breaks in with Blue Jean Baby, crooning

like an absolute angel, then lets it go . . .
straight-ahead bop. Radio: red light of what remains
just talk till evening.

Bird on the Motif of Lemons

Raised as you were, you cannot know
the lightness a mother feels bearing her child,
letting go that separate, integral thing.
Nature screams for harvest, allows no time
for metaphor. Fruit rots in the cellar. A thousand
breasts, two by two, walk the town square each night.
Do you think the tree cries losing its blossom?
It is glad to be rid of it, the way our swollen bellies feel
good against one another, as if we haven't lost anything,
as if, in this world, there is only gain, only mountains.

Bird on What Must Be Broken

We share a ruin—mine a pinprick burrowed
in the side of this hardwood column,
yours a shuttered room in a crumbling mission.
The whole city's an imperfect thing—the cars
slow to fire, the black-trousered men
painstaking in their exits. If you could
use your hands, if your hands held
the enviable knowledge a woman feels
when she screams with joy, if they could
touch that machinery . . . The old bricks
falling off the hotel wait for the mason,
from whose rough hands they learned trust.
Repair a thing and it's yours forever.

Back Home, Grandfather Falls. Except in Pictures

Back home, Grandfather falls. Except in pictures,
the fishermen no longer fish their sacred lake.
Still the days are filled with impatiens and hostas,
the beds newly mulched. The first and only time
my father came to Mexico we spoke the future of the farm
over dinner. It seemed unfashionable, beside the gazebo,
under the harbor's bright lights—the first time
he ordered the words *blessing* and, unbelievably, *arrival in itself.*
Thus uttered, Bird moves to prove these absolutes:
A man ruins himself working the ground, loves most
a furrowed face. Quiz: *Do you recognize me? Father, how
many moons? Whose lackluster color? Mine? The Old Man
in the Moon's? Wild mustard's . . . . Dill's?* Tables
turned, for once waxing, I climb question marks'
humped backs, hang on, up and down, steady as I plow
those great swells Grandfather called his bread and butter
for lack of better.

Interlude
for Love & Mortification

Bird on Somnambulism

Your father, a father, anyone's father, went out in it—
morning: and there was no greater glory than to see,
alongside him, that first world. This was the realm of
fathers, the soil work of memory. What father knows
blanketing the green fields each night with his
pressing body . . . Work! Grow tired! Carry on!
When I come to you over this labyrinthine city,
notice I come early in the cool wet rain.
The sun brightens, makes a show of itself. Risen with it,
I share the same house, have occupied it, in fact,
since the beginning.

The fifth grade, mostly Anglo, mostly angelic, leans in, listens
to the town prodigal: the wonderbeast I have become,
revisiting my alma mater. The kids in back point, misbehave,
this being social studies, this being June, this being the word
freak tossed about in the room between summer's sprawl
and school's strict accounting. I sound serious tones of villages
minus fathers, grandfathers, whole towns abandoned, imagine,
for Tucson, for dollars. The poverty of others slides off them
like sweat, like threats heard around the dinner table, like dumb
ear holes swirled into wood, like all truths, beyond hearing.
In their comfortable skins—their mothers' blue eyes
and their fathers' capital bodies—Bird flies home on the strength
of Grandfather's good world: delicious breeding, fair schools,
the promise of land that delivers. I was along for those rides.
I was a little harvester. I augured the incredible. Never
did it occur to me that my family wasn't the richest, luckiest
in town or anywhere—not, in those days, freaks, but fixtures.
So when I climbed down the combine's ladder and ran home
through the husks' shucked remains—those were stories
without really being stories, the old joke where the kid slips
gum out of its wrapper, chews its contents, then puffs
the still-sweet wrapper up for offer.

◧

I return a falcon-headed god, a wonderbeast, a blaze
of feathers brazen around my neck, eye-liner dragged
above my eye-whites, the carnal, world-eating beak.
My bug-eyes sweep the ground to find it brittle, brown.
Believe it? I knock the way the farm kids did, broken down
on their way to work, hazy mornings, my grandmother
the only one up. I had not forgotten. I knew the farm by heart.
My grandfather, who once looked guileless lads up and down,
saying nothing, now does the same with me, considering
another in a history of door-to-door solicitous geeks:
politicians/rednecks/salesmen/priests. We talk weather,
eyeball the rain gauge he suspects emblematic—how you check
a fuel tank or bathroom scale—sigh with relief or hell.

Like Khrushchev in the Great Plains, all I could do was grumble
and eat and shit and laugh. It did, didn't it, grow ridiculous—
this great beast of a man, this circumstantial mute, ruminating
on the monstrosity of an American farm. Whatever
knowledge I had of other worlds rested squarely
on my tongue. Drought had left a sad film at the rain gauge
high-water mark, the long-ago meniscus you once duplicated
for Grandfather after school, when he feigned surprise, made
transparent comments like, *Why do you suppose it does that* or
I'll be damned. That was seminal, you want to tell him—
the two of you talking like strangers—that was childhood,
the first and last time you could command such wonders.

Do I want to come inside, Grandfather asks, maybe
sit down a spell, get some news. *Yes.* I resolve
to spare this good man no natural wonder. I pass
a field's length of barbed wire through my tongue.
I raise the dried bones of the old dead, reoccupy,
finally, my landed body. In return, I see only
the television's twin blue pyramids reflected
in his eyeglasses, a five o'clock news blur
of djinni and anchorman. A look slants my way,
by way of assurance. I could see, couldn't I,
how it had to do with food? A gesture towards the tube,
where Khrushchev, flickering, strides down the chrome
swirl of the milk aisle at a San Francisco grocery,
disbelieving. What a rube! And Nikita's own brand
of indignation—priceless—when first he lays
eyes on a middle American kitchen. *Impossible,*
he grouses, suspecting a Yank plot: refrigeration,
tin can openers—all touch-of-a-button.

■

For dinner, we turn to the sweetcorn patch, farmer and
wonderbeast posed fresh for some fabulist's idea of a new
American Gothic. He chooses his best dozen, stripping them
down to the waist like an army recruiter: firm squeeze
and chuck into the grocery bag's cut mouth I am all too glad
to hold open. Pass or Fail. Satisfactory or Not. American or un-
American. Smart snap of ears broken from stalks, clean rip
of husks unsheathed, hard luck assessments of the misshapen
and stunted. Unmasked, the wonderbeasts we become.

The Woman, Dr. Perez Asks, Indicating Esperanza

The woman, Dr. Perez asks, indicating Esperanza in the lobby,
is that your mother? Upon further review, I tell him, the image
of a nursing breast in the examination room cannot be
a Mexican breast. More likely it's an Amherst breast, but a breast
all the same. Mother! Cubs! I embody *hysteric*, flop on the exam
room table like a salmon for you, Doctor. Oh my heart! My life!
I have the most pressing questions: Why the monk on the pulp
fiction jacket should tug the g-string off a paperback dancer.
If boys clip my heels on the way home whistling Stars 'n Stripes,
should I salute them, hum along through my tongue depressor?
Don't, the good doctor interrupts, *punish yourself. Go school shopping.*
You will feel better, a folder in which to place everything, an uncluttering.
You are in danger, he intones, tripping headlong over his English,
of seeing all loves as the same dirty classroom. So the mind goes
like this, he says, letting slip from his desk desire's unruled pages.

As It Is Necessary for the Physician to Possess Perfect

As it is necessary for the physician to possess perfect
knowledge of remedies and maladies in order to apply to each
of the latter that which tends to counteract it, so I took it upon myself
to be their true physician, to live purely and without such excess. I read
Father Diego's missionary pages straight from his journal.
Priest-holed, Bird listens, cuts his teeth on the monkish
dialectic. Off with his head!, he screams. Socrates,
he careens the room deep in thought, intercepting insects,
manna en route. You must, Bird adds, take nothing on faith.
I have diagnosed in you ailments of the heart needing
rectification, soup and/or gelatin. Consider the case
forthcoming in my *Book of Desires*: Suppose
the merchant Caxines and the tailor Alexos de Pastrama
arrange for a year of "services" from the Captain's wife
at a cost of 24 ducados. The Captain fails to deliver. What
is your ruling? Bird eyes me critically. I hem and haw, seeking
a way out of his syllogism, the way Bird complains
the mission windows make the argument *clarity=passage*; ergo
passage=windows. And yet there, Bird says, he runs amuck.
Time! he shouts, where love is a TV quiz show, and
tomorrow brings news of a game show scandal blown
so wide open no one believes it, having taken the crude
intellectual drama behind glass as absolute.

Last Night in the Cosmic Silence Glassblowers Say Exists

Last night in the cosmic silence glassblowers say exists
only in Tibet, I met two friends. Still seeing that temptress,
I asked Francisco, the cheesemaker, who once used her
bathtub as his milk separator. No, but he had run into her,
he said, the break-up had been recent, and I could tell—
he told me as much—he had buried his fingernails over it.
Not to worry, old friend, I said, the ancient Sun was a huge orb
batted about the heavens. The Moon, as you already know,
is green cheese. And you, Esperanza, I said, turning to my sweet
and lovely friend, have you any quandaries? Will you throw this
brie into the air and catch it exactly? She did, albeit obligatorily,
like an organ she had ground a thousand times. I could see
then her face fill out, deepen. We didn't know how, suddenly,
Francisco and I, to vie for this earth mother's attentions,
but began by batting about a fiery ball of Agave roots. As rivals
contest, I am told, so did we, at dusk, uneclipsed.

One Learns Not to Ask Certain Things

One learns not to ask certain things.
Why 6:45 a.m.—the stones in the street
unwarmed—why, off the coast,
an epicenter, why, overhead, chandeliers?
Why the partial mudslide, so the streets
the morning after looked like a science fiction.
The traffic cop, my favorite apparition—
with his gold teeth, round shades and leer—
beats all; he's a lightning rod of humanity
in the earthquake's aftermath, gliding from
corner to corner while snakeskins steep in oil,
as usual. I do not ask for answers, for formulas.
I feel the brush across the boot's burnished globe,
I look down.

For the First Time I Find the Cold Invigorating

For the first time I find the cold invigorating,
the door ajar in absentmindedness—as if the mission
house had gone out and forgotten its shawl.
The whitewash, the clearly framed doors . . . It had,
up till now, been immaculate.

Beneath the chandelier, the earth moved,
choked at its chains. Father Diego, with his shuffling
feet and razored head, hastened to examine the hail-strafed
maidenhairs, defrocked impatiens.
He found me in my wormwood room. Intact.

I had been frozen to the ground in my stocking feet.
I had seen clearly, to Bird's chagrin, the mind of winter.
Then the outside became the inside. I felt my feet,
if they needed a reason, would go colorless
when I demanded of them, Why the change?

After Diego went and before Cat braved roof again,
I wanted to know, for drama's sake, Why
couldn't it have been grapefruit-sized hail, like Texas?
Had it been, I felt confident the windows would have revealed,
under duress, the heat of their origins.

The Moon, Long-Mustachioed and Lashed, Ate the Sun

The moon, long-mustachioed and lashed, ate the sun.
Night fell. The fire first refused to catch then cracked with fat.
Why should I be so lucky? The water in the bowl
warmed to skin's touch, my mattress firm as Goat's.
Even Moth, paper-thin, hazards the cold outside the flu.

The old wood explodes in a thousand places. Riddled
with holes, everything's older and lighter than imagined.
Otherwise, I might never have started off, the bag I shoulder
so small. I drift towards sleep, as towards a succulent
sheep's tail—like some children do, imagining myself

sans spectacles, ascending some saddleback street in some woolly
Western vest. Something different about him, people would say,
as behind me a hillside city cascades towards a sacred lake.
Then my eyes, too, grow heavy with imagining, and nightsmoke
carries me over the mission's tiled roof.

And what I come down to finally is a softness: the brown,
essential earth, a transcript of a first love poem, a suggestion
of leaves and fruit—the last fir cut in the distance
and Bird's return just after, all these things . . . and the seed-
bearing silk fallen in the stone yard.

All Day the Twin Brothers Swap Chainsaw Parts

All day the twin brothers swap chainsaw parts.
Wordlessly. Nothing I can utter, nothing
I can say when the motor whines again

with its nervous brain. If I were likewise handy,
I would talk Sheep out of his skin, make noise
around town, his shorn tail between my legs.

I would, and listen: terra cotta rubs my stockings red.
Kiss: It is an exhalation, a something I cannot tell you,
not from here, not with my hands, not in this skin.

Conquistador:
A Masquerade in Four Parts

I concede the rain as that further, expected
deprivation. Still the sky is mine, *Conquistador's*.
I claimed, at least, a sizable chunk. Rain or no,
penitents arrive, take the whole church nave
on their knees. Their healing, when it comes,
sounds to my ears like stone splitting water.
I watch, far away, their cloud of spirits.
A long, long time ago . . ., I sing. Oh, a sailor
and his solitude!

+

Turn off the cell phone, bring out the alms,
man of god, I'm drying up! The chocolates I bought
last Tuesday have made me splendid. What I'd give
for a little romp beneath the bougainvillea.
My dreams, *senors*, *senoras*, have been touched
with licentiousness. I've rubbed against the pillow,
the mattress. I've dipped into the unclean river, come
up with the rough sinews of a basketball net. At long last,
Sparrow flits from lemon to lemon, bickering
with his girlfriend. He is unsettled, hops after me
in a rain of crumbs. All day long I've been a fat,
Franciscan friar leaving the pie plates out, licking
the sweet mango off my lips.

✝

I am sick for love, having spent too long
in this country's Vulcan heart, too long
at the newsstand firing my loins.
In my youth, I lusted after the daughters
of kings, loved them who would never love back.
It seemed the right discipline.
And when finally I reached those unfamiliar
shores, I did not drink enough, did not lie
long on the beach, did not become
a charmer of hymens as the kings might have
instructed: *Show my daughters how it feels*
to have their wombs turned inside out.
Their liquory baritones in every conch.

✝

I grow tired of navigating the wine-dark sea
by night, the world by questions: *Which way
to the Yucatan? To the Silk Fields? The Gold Mines?*
I ask, receive a litany of recovered truths,
seeds pulled from a sullen river. In time, Eros
makes us mad. We come to the sea to wash,
stare at our bodies, quicksilver beneath the water, think,
what pale fruit; at the marble sky, shake fists, say,
Look here. See this? In time, grapes are picked. Vines
learn absence. It is a cruel game Fox must play.
No one knows whether, returning to the sea, he starves
from cunning or from pride. No one imagines,
when he drowns, how easily his stars pass for light.

Bird on Lesser Gods

It might be worth your knowing
the lesser gods of grievance:
the three-naveled goddess of afternoon
talk show preemption, the patron saint
of canceled flights to warmer places.
That way, given two tasks of ontological
urgency to do at once—mend a raven
in a ruined courtyard, say, fence-in,
a loud but oracular wolfhound—you
wouldn't anger the pantheon. But suppose
the wolfhound escapes as you walk out
the door to catch your flight to rendezvous
with the raven, which god should you petition:
the god of immaculate reconciliation
or the Mycenaeans' Mistress of Animals.
And would either consider the swollen apple
of your confusion adequate compensation?
Something tells me it might be worth
your knowing the Haitian *loa*, worth
your finding out whether they really speak
desire to serpents in the great ocean and
in what tongue.

Tonight, at the Hotel Fiesta, I Shall Shine with Mescal

Tonight, at the Hotel Fiesta, I shall shine with mescal,
I will wield it like a captain in (what else?) his quarters.
I will be above irony or below it . . . in short, willing.
Twelve guitars will seem the perfect number.
(Raise the red flag! Her hand on the back of his
green felt fedora, pulling down, his nose plumbing
her breasts and the *campaneros* smoking, through it all,
the honeycomb of lust!). Breezes, have you no heart
for endurance, the slow bend of fine-bone, *carpals, meta-*
carpals cupped in surf, the perfectly agreeable wrist? No then,
I, your captain, supped somewhere in between
ocean and stars: a little water, a little good salt:
woman, perfect in this half-light.

Christ in the Square Touches Them Like a Flower

Christ in the square touches them like a flower,
When he is through, the crowd claps meekly,
and the man who smells of my grandfather
gets up. Christ goes on waving, but nobody
recognizes him. For this, I am strangely,
unaccountably glad. His passion play made
the shoe-shining stop, made benches roll over,
arrested the oily seas inside Coke bottles.
The American starlet, teasing her hair, picks up
the applause. The way Lizard remembers Sun,
I return to the mission smelling of it—boot balms,
mink oil, shoebrush. Everyone must see the next step
I'd taken towards baptism. I'd be considered equal
among the men in from the country—
saddle-worn, slump-backed, but shoe-polished—
and their dogs, who now and then raise their hackles,
cow the bitches down.

We Are Always More or Less in Love with the Musician

We are always more or less in love with the Musician,
whose improvisations, like the sea's, please everyone.
Esperanza, too . . . the giddiness of her laughter ringing
the too-loud walls when, with guitar, Diego knocks for tea.
I am gardening for her though, still sacrificing
my afternoons for her warm sun, my hands
standing in for scythe in the head-tall grass.

I am making order with all the indignation of a snubbed god,
Why should every night be a singing night, I ask, leaving
the roses less than perfect. In a garden of things,
things will never tell you their name (*Poinsettia!*),
so sit in silence, pretend the underbelly of things holds
no mystery, no radiant, unsuspected light.

Diego, invisible behind the wall, strums.
The clothes on the line hold their agreed-upon shape.
Overtures drift into evening. Most of what I've heard
I misunderstand. Having no idea where it comes from,
I sit beneath the tree's straightest spire and watch
Columbine purple the wall.

Then it comes to me . . . the first, nameless
fruit of the season. A sweet accumulation
of words—themselves, enlarging and receding
like ships—make loved ones strangers.
I have made this place, this far off plot, home
among ghosts, settled.

I have witnessed many perfect days I wouldn't speak of
back home, where the world's other perfect days
must be had. Some tell me, Stay! Put down
responsibility's books! I wonder if my own father
would recognize me, or if, in my unrecognizability,
I am the crux of something new.

By Dusk My Breath Comes in Rushes. I Am Triumphant

By dusk my breath comes in rushes. I am triumphant
with my handful of blooms. *See Esperanza? See?*
Bittersweet. I trace the wet stone path back
to the mission. Moth, alongside, twirls madly
into it—the dim a visitor expects, arriving late,
their hosts long intertwined. Twilight grows
noise a thousandfold—the drawn bath a waterfall,
the phone an unconscionable alarm—causing the lovers,
each in their separate dream, to stir, see, moving
towards them, an old friend with an empty pale
and fistful of flowers. *Thank you for these blooms*
of unexpected coming, they say, ghosts in nightclothes.
Thank you for your lack of tooth, my friend, they add,
cooing in the same breath, *almost.*

Bird on Other Worlds

I don't know much about Guatemala, or plum trees,
but I feel I can speak confidently on how nighties behave
in open air, how the white light above the cheesemaker's *House of*
Always Brie turns blue at the corner of *Virgin Guadalupe*. Not much
beyond that: the harbor's dirty wash, the violent shimmer
of almost-summer in the atlases, in the mountains, the one good
road there, the two sequined peaks, three maybe five hundred
miles away, by car, their shudder and ripple. From there,
depend on the rug merchant, yawning beneath the plum tree,
to weave you a tale, unfold you a map.

Interlude

for Love & Arms

❂ *Interlude for Love and Arms* ❂

Postcard 1918: Nights Grandmother and kid pilots
everywhere tuned voices deep in sleep's dive and roll,
imagined themselves to be their mothers putting out
victory gardens. Conception married obligation, carried
orders to be filled years later: *Food for Peace, Marshall Plan*.
Root, flour, fruit dropped from heavy skies, pregnant planes.
Operation Vittles, Operation Manna. Enough for pilots, enough
for armies, enough for sons, who, once lost en route,
found sky was neither lover nor Other, but space
from which to say, *enough red earth, enough mother.*

✦

Postcard 1937: Some things Grandfather felt—pain of noon
blistering the courthouse, bankers married to their awnings, loam
on his teeth on the tractor, the smallness of men. He had no use
for religion, but liked the way the chapel looked in the twilight:
the vining mortar, the long windows shaped like bishops. Like
monsters. His eyes followed them upward.

✪

Postcard 1943: Marriage's first days, its very first days.
Grandmother listens to his talk of farming, listens to it deep
in his throat. A benevolence he cannot understand, she dazzles,
she so quietly dazzles him. She brings it to him. At three. She sits
with him. His thermos of coffee, Yuban. Her raven hair and
white skin. Their purposeful swallowing, and afterwards
the whole room smelling of coffee and chewing gum.
His veins would rise when she ran the soap over them,
his veins would rise and lather would run white on his dark skin.
She would shine like daylight. Like daylight for him.

The Web Frames the Lime with Its Perfect Garland

The web frames the lime with its perfect garland.
Still my sight chides me, Move from still-life!
Today is the Festival of Webs and Widows,
the Day of Spider, who respectfully declines.
She and I wait out the parade in her honor,
walls crumbling, the mayor's key to the city fingered
by a thousand, less palpable hands. We spend
the afternoon in the company of bees, whose
confidence allows we frame, *au precise*, the well-
hung fruit. Still-life: that Spider be
what she has always been. That I rail, darken,
browbeat, and she weaves and jigs. That I forget
what happened under other moons, in other cities:
loves the soul didn't love. Entanglements, hot seasons.
Silk so thick it buried, blanketed the tongue.
Campaign: More rain for the leaves! More light
for the maidenhairs! Platform: May you build
always your outrageous house. Rally: In the corner,
in the fashion of my good and undone heart.

After Diego Reclaimed His Basketball—Retreating

After Diego reclaims his basketball—retreating
to higher ground—I roll lemons into the well-troweled
holes Esperanza made. This game precedes wind-sprints
the way a super cool wind precedes rain. The roof
I climb because I need to know what it looks like
from up there: my world in microcosm, my charming
little mission. In a single bound I become *Senor Apetito*
Con Gusto: Mr. Big Lusty Appetite Man, Mexican superhero.
I should tell you the whole thing falls through:
the roof's half-fired tiles crumbling underfoot.
The afternoon begs for replacement. *It is a romance*
of the insane to make work for themselves, I declare, suddenly
Mr. Fix It. Again, I can't say if Bird's acrobatics make him
the most arrogant of aviators or simply the greatest showman,
though I am certain his heart beats quicker than mine
and that he is more or less alone.

Diego's Voice, the First Time Heard outside the Mission

Diego's voice, the first time heard outside the mission,
sounds tinny. Removed of Esperanza's influence,
it swells and breaks in the hotel chapel with all
the pomp and machismo as befits the cavernous:
Only civil beings possess political rights. God's grace is God's law.
But my peasant heart makes claims! I want to pipe up,
though to do so would be to interrupt, sweep
the pulpit from under him and turn his dulcet
histories (*The natives ruled as gods and yet, by cause
of their irrationality, turned lawless.*) to my own
dubious wonderings. Bird appears then, drunk.
Tourists laugh, point, as he flits in and out of holes
no bigger than my thumb. I say, Behold!
For he must be a god who makes a home
of so many small places.

Smoke Appears against the Mountain

Smoke appears against the mountain,
the slow recounting of the unmentionable
to the lips, the *yes* preceding all forgetting:
the taste of chicken cooked by a woman stripped
down to her underwear on the city's outskirts—
wash day—beyond the church, beyond the hospital,
laundering against the sky. In the market, the blue
tarps open again like memory after a darkening.
Renewed, the old lamp (such stirring curves!) turns
suddenly saleable. Hand-wringing, the widower-
owner of the *groceria* oils finally his sliding ladders.
Now, he's up and down all night, searching
for tins. Everyone's open for business.
So when do I stop pressing my feet for revelations?
When do I stop playing matador to every sidewalk crack?
Leave the door open, and all humanity tumbles in.
Closed, it's solemn as a graveyard.

Bird on Fisher Kings

Somehow Fish knows—your needfulness
a halo seen from underwater—Stay away!
Why kick the pier with your wane
knees dangling, why continue that way
until the last motorboat leaves, over-
flowing with tourists. Your hands remain
knotted in your pockets, speaking of their own
misfortunes, expecting Worm to reciprocate.
Remember catching the yellow butterflies
beside childhood's deep well? Your mother had it,
if you rubbed their wings, they would never fly.
There would be a strict accounting. So you imagined
a bank ledger of the touched. Thus,
her math proved false when the sky above
your sixth year became a snowglobe, only
in reverse, a paper-thin iridescence rising, left
and right, from your still disbelieving hands.

Interlude
for Love & Espionage

Interlude for Love and Espionage

Postcard 1955: an incendiary year in the *Register*,
claiming Ike and the man who threatened to bury the whole
shootin' match ought to settle it, instead, like chaps,
on the cornfield—see who could raise the greatest yields,
all things being equal. But they weren't equal,
and Grandfather, who rooted always for the underdog,
packed his bags for Coon Rapids, Iowa, curious to see
the face of Khrushchev, the Russian wonderbeast. Truth is,
he wanted to plow through and bend the Chairman's ear
to the idea of a morning drive, just the two of them.
He would explain along the way the sacred science
of hybrids and, by virtue of his yeoman's knowledge
of this most esoteric of arts, find himself ingratiated.
Reality was, scribblers crowded his gig, so close
to the proverbial trough all he could make out
was the hawkish profile of millionaire farmer-host
Roswell Garst shooing reporters away with cornstalks.
Grandfather captured all this in his trusty seedcorn
notebook—one of many liberated from headquarters—
and stowed in the shed's defunct deep-freeze, where last year's
apples waited, greenly persuaded of cold wars to follow.

Postcard 1959: There's Khrushchev and there's grandfather,
photographed together in cosmic conjunction. Grandfather's
staring off newsprint's ragged edge into starry margins,
an ah-shucks gawk on his face, one vascular hand dipped
into the wagon's Eisenhower-era corn wealth. Khrushchev,
foreground's child, palms the prize ear by the husk,
dumbfounded, as if, once and for all, size would matter.
The world was opening then, slowly, the bald globe
of the Chairman's head spinning on its axis, facing
seedcorn king and superhost Garst in surprise, even
suspicion, the polished heads of KGB brass orbiting.
Whatever gravity moved the crowd to look, along with
my grandfather, away from the camera at that moment,
away from history's counterfeit, had the power of epiphany:
epaulets, bibs, pinstripes—all did an about-face.

P.S.: Imagine the photo taken that afternoon as a clock's face,

the *Register's* newspaper editor advised, a decision nearing

when he would choose to run either grandfather's integral world,

local color, or a shot of the two great men cropped to suggest

weighty isolation. History—*humph*—once developed, turned out

little more than a team pic: the ball dropped and the kids looking

slant. In the end, history ran at wide angle, *as is*—

my grandfather and his ilk, horn-rimmed and long-suffering;

Khrushchev and Garst alone, at three o'clock, with the bullhorn.

Postcard 1960: The question became *what is the nature*
of refreshment each time the commercial came on where
the hard bodies sipped space age brew and let slip
into a scintillating Nestea plunge. The other one was:
Who are you working for, though, on principle, Grandfather refused
to ask it each noon at the table. Still, kid pilots everywhere
wondered about wrestling one down in town, a Communist
given away by doomsday count or nervous tic—payback
for Francis Powers, Ike's U-2 fall guy, tried and sentenced
to ten years for a few innocent pics. It all had to do with envy,
Grandfather said, how having the best of everything insured
enemies. Surely they could see, couldn't they? But by that time
kid pilots everywhere were glued to the tube, committed
to learning trust back first. Mid-plunge day after day (*mayday!*),
bedposts proved apt deterrent. They wore red badges for months
and trademark shiners slowed by bags of Birdseye peas and
Bomb Pops. They stayed on base, close to home, avoiding
photographs, Howard Hughes-like, in long-sleeved Superman
shirts and dead giveaway home cuts, buzz jobs all later agreed
had been frighteningly too close.

Bird Opposing Middle America

Waspish farm wives and woodcuts of bent-
over gardeners in bloomers; farmers tipping
seedcorn caps from cab tractors
slicing soil to bone. Home: where
The Book of Desires opens automatically
each night to the phrase—*ye must*—etched
in penance. What lover doesn't read
that page, bolt upright in bed, cold
lump in their throat, the dogs outside howling,
obscene. Obligation becomes the intellect's
flatline dictatorship, an exile from the heart's
persistent upswell. Should you live
among people who treat gods as mountains,
you shall be breathless, like the sanctuary's
chiseled savior, alive in the gloam.

Bird with Twenty Questions

What's the worst you've been accused of.
Do you like the name *Guy*. At a yard sale,
do you price to move. Would you make love
in a manger. Do you fall asleep at dinner.
Have you ever lodged a pencil in a ceiling. What
would you do in Cuba, with Castro. When dancing
are you nervous for your feet. Is your shadow
pleasing. If so, how much (how many)
ferns have died in your care. Do dwarfs unsettle.
Do you have a daughter. What physical defect
do you find unbearable in a lover. Have you ever
nursed a squirrel back to health with an eye-dropper.
What happened. Do you like the idea of yourself
in a convertible. Have you ever purposefully undressed
in front of a window. Do you hear things. In your opinion,
how many shots rang out from behind the grassy knoll.
Are you, Sweet Conspiracy, acting alone?

I Would Want for the Thunder to Echo, for My Family

I would want for the thunder to echo, for my family
to be almond-eyed and olive-complected—impossibly small,
even thin-skinned, a minor exporter of sadness.
How easily I would milk them of their secrets, make sangria
of counter-intelligence! Home under an umbrella of immunity,
I would read propaganda into passing faces, find my face,
fulsome face, framed in a pool of crude and rainwater.
In the back room afterwards, then, always under a bare bulb,
the music of glad knives! The family calls for the butcher's son,
the joyous, careless one. From his knife milk flows
even in the direction of dissidents.

The Retired General Still Wears His Fatigues

The retired General still wears his fatigues,
if only secretly, if only in the so-called *war room*.
The kiss of mortality feels to him like someone (his wife?)
touching his ear, urging him back. Impossible . . .
singing to the general in his bloodlust! Like waking up
in a quiet coastal town, like looking across the Gulf
at waves building like violent headlines, you return
to your own body, itself an unknown country
occasioned by unrest, peopled by inequities,
where tennis is played by the wealthy, but not
in the day's heat, which represents a kind of brutality.
So often a mission gets spent doing something else—
reading the newspaper—though it occurs to you:
This work is important. This work must get done.
At that pronouncement, irascible Spider, who doesn't,
judging from its markings, know whether it's coming
or going, rears up. Do not misunderstand. It is a struggle
of universal needs. Who shall have the leftover fruit?
I empty the plate and hope for a stalemate.

Only Lovers in the Churchyard Warm the Face of Death

Only lovers in the churchyard warm the face of death.
Four a.m. and the archangel's wings are drenched in gasoline.
The coins in the beggar's cup glow with fire.
In a barrage of kissing, bangs are brushed back.
The nuns keep close in their quiet rooms, careful not to wake
the dogs in the cool of the nave. Only the children
have offhand conversations with god, in the foyer, to the point
of distraction. Forgetting to cross themselves, they move forward,
while the lovers pepper one another with their small, sincere gifts.
The Sanctuary's blue-lit staves suggest hospital. Inspire.
Otherwise day's a ruin. The blind accordionist picks the shop
marked *Optica*; the eye importunes the heart, not the Other.
What plays in his eye bones? *Tormenta. Storm-swirl.* The night
spins down especially cold—and possible. Unmuddied—
clean and possible—struck at even, longed for.

Though It Frightens Me, the Bees Slide in the White Folds

Though it frightens me, the bees slide in the white folds,
the blossoms, at work. Outside, the waiting taxi stays faithful.
While the bees shake hands, backslap, my fears branch
and bear fruit. Esperanza's bronzed hand clutches the trowel.
I mouth a thousand phrase book mantras: *It was very good.*
It looks like rain. It was a fair price. Goodbye. Esperanza, inside
I am writing for you a handsome farewell poem, a handsome
farewell poem stars Tom Selleck as swashbuckling revolutionary.
I am making for you a dangerous farewell poem featuring
a botched CIA invasion of a burning island. I am thinking:
Why not end in flames. I am thinking of disappearance
and Tom Selleck, of you and I, arm in arm, as the news
reaches us. Then I am thinking of poems again, and Bird,
who understands perfectly the inanity of music
and wings.

About the Author

ZACHARY MICHAEL JACK is the author of the fine arts poetry chapbook *The Story of Grief* from Oeoco Press (2000) and the editor of two essay collections *Black Earth and Ivory Tower: New American Essays from Farm and Classroom* and *The Furrow and Us: Essays on Soil and Sentiment*. His poetry has earned him the Prentice Hall Poetry Prize, a nomination for a Pushcart (Best of the Small Presses) Prize and writing residencies at New York's Blue Mountain Center and Ireland's Tyrone Guthrie Centre, among others. A native of Iowa, Jack is an assistant professor of English at North Central College in Naperville, Illinois and the director-founder of the School of Lost Arts for children.

About the Publication

Founded in 2004, New Buffalo Press draws its inspiration from the dramatic meeting of land and water along Michigan's southwestern shores, its dunesland. A member of the Independent Book Publisher's Association (PMA), New Buffalo typically publishes poets by invitation, actively seeking visionary work with a narrative impulse. In keeping with its mission, NBP maintains an open reading period for unsolicited manuscripts postmarked during the month of August. Because New Buffalo seeks to produce volumes of artistic as well as literary merit, the press encourages submissions exclusively from poets with existing working relationships with professional book designers and presses and from exceptional poets with the ability to write as well as design books beautifully.

The text of these poems has been set in Baskerville; Adobe Caslon semibold italic and Cochin italic have been used for titles and section breaks. Images used in this book appear from the *Big Box of Art* produced by Hemera Techologies Incorporated of Canada.

Notes

"As It Is Necessary for the Physician to Possess a Perfect": The quote attributed to the fictional Father Diego is adapted from the great sixteenth-century Franciscan ethnographer Bernardino de Sahagun's work *Historia general de las cosas de Nueva Espana* as quoted in Bernardino Verastique's fine history of Western Mexico *Michoacan and Eden* (University of Texas Press, 2000). The real-life case of Baptista Caxines and Alexos de Pastrama, abbreviated and adapted in the poem, is also detailed in Veratisque's book.

"Diego's Voice, the First Time Heard outside the Mission": In the poem, Father Diego gives voice to a sentiment regarding *dominium* common among missionaries in Western Mexico, including bishop and judge Don Vasco De Quiroga (1477/78–1565). According to Veratisque, Quiroga did employ a "strongman" by the name of Father Diego, though the character by that name in the poem is purely fictional.

"In the Cosmic Silence Glassblowers Say Exists Only in Tibet": The narrator references a view of the Purhepecha Indian cosmos which held that the Sun was a kind of cosmic pinball; the game played by the narrator and Francisco in the poem's last line is based on a myth-derived game still played with maguey roots.

"Interlude for Love and Espionage": Though Khrushchev and Garst did meet publicly in Coon Rapids, certain elements of their meeting have been fictionalized.

General Disclaimer: Any resemblance between the fictional characters in these poems and real persons is purely coincidental.

77

Bird Afterword

You never know
what someone is
dog-earing your page
in The Book of Desires
you kept so unassidiously
and with what: lipstick
imprint, lover's spreading
lips, or last preserved flower
full puckered to a kiss.
There must be some slip
of something keeps
your place—orange
rind, guitar pick,
snakeskin saying
double back.

9 781595 409614